TABLE OF CONTENTS

Unless otherwise indicated, all Scripture quotations are taken from the King James Version of the Bible.
7 Hidden Ingredients in Every Miracle
ISBN 1-56394-394-8/B-280 · Copyright © 2007 by **MIKE MURDOCK**
All publishing rights belong exclusively to Wisdom International
Publisher/Editor: Deborah Murdock Johnson
Published by The Wisdom Center · 4051 Denton Hwy. · Ft. Worth, Texas 76117
1-817-759-BOOK · 1-817-759-0300
You Will Love Our Website...! www.TheWisdomCenter.tv

The Harvest
You Have Sown For
Is At Hand.

-MIKE MURDOCK

WHY I WROTE THIS BOOK

This Is A Very Exciting Season Of My Life!

Discerning seasons is critically important. "To everything there is a season and a time to every purpose under the heaven," (Ecclesiastes 3:1). "Then I will give you rain *in due season*, and the land shall yield her increase, and the trees of the field shall yield their fruit," (Leviticus 26:4).

This is your Season of *Miracles.*

On the morning of October 30th, I was awakened by The Holy Spirit to the most extraordinary celebration in my spirit: *"The next 61 days are going to be the greatest season of miracles for the families of those who support and stand with the ministry, The Wisdom Center."*

I knew it would be spectacular!

I knew I was experiencing an Uncommon Visitation of God that special morning. Yet, I did not know the Volcano of Victories that would soon erupt in my spirit.

Immediately, I dressed and drove from my home to The Wisdom Center to meet with my staff and Leadership Team to tell them what The Holy Spirit had birthed in my heart. *Instantly*, they embraced the same revelation and promise.

Miracles are a major part of my Belief System. My life has been filled with miracles...from the age of two and one-half years.

I feel an urgency to share these principles with you: *The Seven Hidden Ingredients Necessary For You*

To Experience A Miracle.

You may say, "Dr. Mike, I don't have enough faith for God to give me a miracle."

As The Holy Spirit is surging within me today, let me boldly state: Your lack of faith does not diminish what I feel for you. I am believing that the faith within me will overcome your doubts and struggles with unbelief. As you read these words, my faith is causing your doubt to *melt like butter in a heated skillet!*

Cancer is *leaving.*

Tumors are *dissolving.*

Poverty is *fleeing.*

Faith is *rising.*

Wayward children are coming *home.*

Family relationships are being *restored.*

By the faith of God, I declare...Doubt is *defeated.*

Explosive faith is flowing from my spirit to yours. God is speaking to you, "The Harvest For Which You Have Sown...Is At Hand."

That is why I wrote this book.

Mike Murdock

≈ 1 ≈
YOU MUST NEED A MIRACLE BEFORE YOU WILL EXPERIENCE ONE

You Cannot Receive From God Until You Reach.

You will not reach for God until you have a desperate need.

What is the greatest *Miracle* you need?

Has someone in your home broken your heart?

Have you lost your job?

Are you facing bankruptcy?

Has the doctor told you there is no hope of healing or a change in your body?

Pursuit Is The Proof Of Desire.

When you really want something, you reach.

Miracles happen *only* for those who seek them.

Bartimaeus *pursued* his Miracle by attracting the attention of Jesus. "Then they came to Jericho. As Jesus and His disciples, together with a large crowd, were leaving the city, a blind man, Bartimaeus (that is, the Son of Timaeus), was sitting by the roadside begging. When he heard that it was Jesus of Nazareth, he began to *shout*, Jesus, Son of David, have mercy on me!" (Mark 10:46-47 NIV).

The hemorrhaging woman *pressed through the crowd* to touch His garment. "And a certain woman, which had an issue of blood twelve years, And had suffered many things of many physicians, and had spent all that she had, and was nothing bettered, but rather grew worse, When she had heard of Jesus, came in the press behind, and touched His garment. For she said, If I may touch but His clothes, I shall be whole. And straightway the fountain of her blood was dried up; and she felt in her body that she was healed of that plague. And Jesus, immediately knowing in Himself that virtue had gone out of Him, turned Him about in the press, and said, Who touched My clothes? And His disciples said unto Him, Thou seest the multitude thronging Thee, and sayest thou, Who touched Me? And He looked round about to see her that had done this thing. But the woman fearing and trembling, knowing what was done in her, came and fell down before Him, and told Him all the truth. And He said unto her, Daughter, thy faith hath made thee whole; go in peace, and be whole of thy plague," (Mark 5:25-34).

Use Your Faith To Get What You Want From God. NOT whining and complaining. "Ask, and it shall be given you; seek, and ye shall find; knock, and it shall be opened unto you: For every one that asketh receiveth; and he that seeketh findeth; and to him that knocketh it shall be opened," (Matthew 7:7-8).

You Must Expect A Divine Reaction...To A Passionate Request. "If a son shall ask bread of any of you that is a father, will he give him a stone? or if he ask a fish, will he for a fish give him a serpent? Or if he shall ask an egg, will he offer him a scorpion? If ye then, being evil, know how to give good gifts unto your children: how much more shall your heavenly Father give the Holy Spirit to them that ask Him?" (Luke 11:11-13).

Conversations reveal expectations.

You Must Need A Miracle Before You Will Experience One.

≈ 2 ≈

YOU NEED A PLEADER, A HUMAN INTERCESSOR, TO STAND IN AGREEMENT WITH YOU

Your Pleader Must Be Someone God Respects.

Abraham pleaded with God for the preservation of Sodom and Gomorrah. "Then the Lord rained upon Sodom and upon Gomorrah brimstone and fire from the Lord out of heaven; And he overthrew those cities, and all the plain, and all the inhabitants of the cities, and that which grew upon the ground. But his wife looked back from behind him, and she became a pillar of salt. And Abraham gat up early in the morning to the place where he stood before the Lord: And he looked toward Sodom and Gomorrah, and toward all the land of the plain, and beheld, and, lo, the smoke of the country went up as the smoke of a furnace. And it came to pass, when God destroyed the cities of the plain, that *God remembered Abraham*, and sent Lot out of the midst of the overthrow, when he overthrew the cities in the which Lot dwelt," (Genesis 19:24-29).

God remembered Abraham...and saved Lot. Lot was saved from judgment by the *pleading* of Abraham!

Lot simply had...a Respected *Pleader.*

The Apostle Peter was arrested and imprisoned for preaching the Gospel. "Peter therefore was kept in prison: *but prayer was made without ceasing of the church unto God for him.* And when Herod would have brought him forth, the same night Peter was sleeping between two soldiers, bound with two chains: and the keepers before the door kept the prison. And, behold, the angel of the Lord came upon him, and a light shined in the prison: and he smote Peter on the side, and raised him up, saying, Arise up quickly. And his chains fell off from his hands," (Acts 12:5-7).

Peter had a group of Pleaders...The Local Church.

Remember when Israel needed an intercessor? None could be found. "And I *sought for a man* among them, that should make up the hedge, and stand in the gap before me for the land, that I should not destroy it: *but I found none,*" (Ezekiel 22:30).

Suffering came to an entire nation because there was no one *Pleading* their case.

I have a personal testimony...about a Pleader. My parents were Pentecostal pioneers who founded seven churches in Texas and Louisiana. Daddy personally built each of the church buildings himself.

At two and one-half years of age, satan attempted to destroy my life. The doctors declared that I was "eaten up" with worms. My mother counted over 600 worms that came out of my body...*in a single day.* Mother even endured the horror of worms crawling out of my mouth onto her shoulder.

The physicians had no cure. Without a miracle, I was going to die.

Mother and Daddy were people who believed God would perform miracles in response to faith. Daddy went into intercession, knelt down and decided he would pray all night, if necessary, for my healing.

He simply lifted his hands and repeated the same

sentence over and over again, *"Thou art a mighty God."*

Within minutes, God gave him a vision of me being held in the arms of satan. In the vision, Jesus calmly walked over and gently took me from the clutches of the devil.

I was healed that very day.

Oh, The Power Of A Pleader!

You Need A Pleader, A Human Intercessor, To Stand In Agreement With You.

Recommended Investments:
B-115 Where Miracles Are Born (32 pages/$5)
B-136 The Wisdom Commentary, Vol. 1 (256 pages/$20)

You Are Never As Far From A Miracle As It First Appears.

-MIKE MURDOCK

❧ 3 ❧

You Must Trust Someone Capable Of Working Miracles

━━━━━━━▶❖◀━━━━━━━

The Dominant Difference In People Is Who They Trust.

Jesus, Our Intercessor, Is A Miracle-Worker.

A Miracle is the supernatural intervention of God into the problems of your life. *A Miracle Is Anything Good That Only God Can Do.* Miracles are often beyond human reasoning or logic. "How God anointed Jesus of Nazareth with the Holy Ghost and with power: who went about *doing good*, and healing all that were oppressed of the devil; for God was with Him," (Acts 10:38).

You have a Miracle-Worker in your life! Jesus! Jesus of Nazareth! Jesus, our Intercessor who sits at the right hand of The Father.

ACCEPT THE UNEXPLAINABLE. Methods will vary. Jesus used *clay and spittle* in healing the blind man near the Pool of Siloam. Jesus used *water pots* to create wine at the marriage celebration in Cana.

Divine methods are often puzzling, unpredictable and *always* illogical to the natural mind of man. "For My thoughts are *not* your thoughts, neither are your ways My ways, saith the Lord. For as the heavens are higher than the earth, so are *My ways higher* than your ways, and My thoughts than your thoughts," (Isaiah 55:8-9). You can pursue any Miracle, *but God chooses The Method* by which He sends it to you.

You Are Never As Far From A Miracle As It First Appears. Today is not permanent. Your worst circumstances today are subject to change...*because* you have a Miracle-Worker in your life.

Your Miracle-Worker's Name Is Jesus.

You are the *creation.*

He is the *Creator.*

He delights in performing the impossible.

Jesus changes *sickness* into *health.*

Jesus changes *poverty* into *prosperity.*

Jesus changes *tears* into *laughter.*

Jesus is the *Master of the Turnaround.* "And Jesus looking upon them saith, With men it is impossible, but not with God: for with God all things are possible," (Mark 10:27).

Let's review the supernatural events in the life of Jesus:

Miracles In The Life Of Jesus

1. **The Supernatural Conception And Pregnancy Of The Virgin Mary.** (See Matt. 1:18-25.)

2. **Wise Men Led To The Birthplace Of Jesus By A Star.** (See Matthew 2:1-9.)

3. **Miraculous Fulfillment Of Prophecy As Jesus Is Born In A Stable.** (See Luke 2:1-7.)

4. **Simeon The Priest Announces The Infant Jesus As The Messiah Of Israel.** (See Luke 2:25-35.)

5. **The Prophetess Anna Declares Baby Jesus To Be The Promised Arrival Of The**

Redeemer Of Mankind. (See Luke 2:36-38.)

6. **Joseph Obeys A Spiritual Dream And Saves The Life Of Mary And The Infant Jesus.** (See Matthew 2:13-23.)

7. **Jesus Astounds The Temple Scholars With His Understanding Of Scripture At The Age Of Twelve.** (See Luke 2:41-49.)

8. **Jesus Works His First Literal Miracle As He Turns Water Into Wine At The Wedding Feast In Cana.** (See John 2:1-11.)

9. **Jesus Heals The Nobleman's Son.** (See John 4:46-54.)

10. **Jesus Gives A Supernatural Instruction That Enables Peter To Catch Two Boat Loads Of Fish.** (See Luke 5:1-7.)

11. **Jesus Issues The Supernatural Call Of Ministry To Simon Peter.** (See Luke 5:8-11.)

12. **Jesus Gives A Second Instruction That Resulted In A Catch Of Fish So Large That It Could Not Be Drawn In.** (See John 21:6.)

13. **A Demonic Delivered In The Synagogue At Capernaum By Jesus.** (See Mark 1:21-27.)

14. **Jesus Heals A Woman Of Demonically Induced Osteoporosis.** (Luke 13:10-17.)

15. **Peter And Andrew Called By Jesus As Fishers Of Men.** (See Matthew 4:18-19.)

16. **Jesus Heals Peter's Mother-In-Law.** (See Matthew 8:14-15.)

17. **Jesus Ministers Deliverance And Healing To Large Crowds Of Followers.** (See Matthew 8:6-17.)

18. **Jesus Cleanses A Leper.** (See Matt. 8:1-4.)

19. **Jesus Heals A Paralytic And Declares**

Healing Is No More Difficult Than Salvation. (See Matthew 9:1-8.)

20. Philip And Nathanael Called To Ministry By The Manifestation Of The Word Of Knowledge Working Through Jesus. (See John 1:43-48.)

21. Jesus Heals A Man At The Pool Of Bethesda Who Had Been Disabled For 38 Years. (See John 5:1-16.)

22. Jesus Heals A Man's Withered Hand On The Sabbath. (See Matthew 12:9-13.)

23. Jesus Heals The Centurion's Servant And Compliments His Understanding Of Spiritual Authority. (See Luke 7:1-10.)

24. Jesus Raises A Widow's Son To Life As He Interrupts A Funeral Procession In Nain. (See Luke 7:11-16.)

25. Jesus Heals A Man By Casting Out A Mute And Blind Spirit. (See Matthew 12:22-37.)

26. Jesus Calms The Storm. (See Matthew 8:23-27.)

27. Jesus Casts Demons Out Of Two Men In Gergesenes. (See Matthew 8:28-34.)

28. Jesus Raises The Daughter Of Jairus From The Dead. (See Matthew 9:18-19; 23-26.)

29. On The Way To Jairus' House, Jesus Heals The Woman With The Issue Of Blood. (See Matthew 9:20-22.)

30. Jesus Restores The Sight Of Two Blind Men. (See Matthew 9:27-31.)

31. Jesus Ministers Healing Through Deliverance To A Mute Demonic. (See Matthew 9:32-33.)

32. Jesus Walks Upon The Waters Of The Sea

Of Galilee. (See Matthew 14:22-33.)

33. Jesus Ministers Deliverance To The Daughter Of The Syrophenician Woman Who Demonstrated Great Faith. (See Matthew 15:21-28.)

34. Jesus Feeds A Crowd Of 5,000 Men And The Thousands Of Women And Children With Them. (See Matthew 14:13-21.)

35. Jesus Heals A Deaf Mute. (See Mk. 7:31-37.)

36. Jesus Heals A Blind Man. (See Mk. 8:22-26.)

37. Jesus Heals Blind Bartimaeus. (See Mark 10:46-52.)

38. Jesus Ministers Deliverance And Heals An Epileptic. (See Matthew 17:14-21.)

39. Temple Tax Money Obtained For Jesus And Peter From A Fish's Mouth. (See Matthew 17:24-27.)

40. Jesus Heals Ten Lepers And Only One Returns To Thank Him. (See Luke 17:11-19.)

41. Jesus Heals A Man Born Blind And Declares Personal Sin Is Not The Cause Of All Illness. (See John 9:1-3.)

42. Jesus Raises Lazarus From The Grave. (See John 11:1-46.)

43. Jesus Heals A Man Of Congestive Heart Failure. (See Luke 14:1-6.)

44. Jesus Restores Sight To Two Blind Men Near Jericho. (See Matthew 20:29-34.)

45. Jesus Condemns A Fig Tree And It Withers. (See Matthew 21:17-22.)

46. Jesus Heals The Ear Of Malchus That Was Cut Off With A Sword By The Apostle Peter. (See Luke 22:49-51.)

47. The Bodily Resurrection Of Jesus

Himself After The Crucifixion And Burial. (See Matthew 28:1-7.)

    48. Jesus Ascends To Heaven And Promises To Come Again To Take Believers Back To Heaven To Live With Him Forever. (See Luke 24:50-51; Acts 1:9-11.)

    Our God is a Miracle God!

    You just read a List of Wonders worked by our Lord Jesus. As impressive as these are, the Apostle John, in his Gospel, makes an even more amazing statement, *"And there are also many other things which Jesus did, the which, if they should be written every one, I suppose that even the world itself could not contain the books that should be written. Amen,"* (John 21:25).

    Believing in the power of God, you have everything to gain and nothing to lose. At *some* point in your life, you will be forced to live in the *potential of your Faith,* or with *the consequences of your Doubt.*

    You Must Have A Miracle-Worker...Someone Capable Of Working Miracles.

❧ 4 ❧
YOU MUST BELIEVE IN YOUR OWN WORTHINESS TO RECEIVE A MIRACLE

You Must Believe You Qualify For A Miracle.

You can only attract what you believe you deserve. You must have faith that the God who invested Jesus in your life at Calvary believes You are worthy of a Miracle.

What was the secret of the little woman who pressed through the crowd to touch the garment of Jesus? She had suffered horribly for 12 years. What motivated her to boldly press her way through the throng?

She believed she was worthy.

She believed she was *qualified* to receive her miraculous healing.

Do you feel *inferior?*

Do you feel *unworthy?*

Do you feel *insignificant?*

Do you feel *no one cares* for you?

If so, you must exert spiritual authority over such thoughts...*or you will die where you are.*

Release a *spirit of boldness* into your life.

You know God. So the supernatural should become habitual in your life. "The people that do know their God shall be strong, and do exploits," (Daniel 11:33).

Jesus Paid A Horrendous Price For You. "For ye are bought with a price: therefore glorify God in your body, and in your spirit which are God's," (1 Corinthians 6:20). This should send a message to you.

Courage changes the seasons of your life.

You Will Need Courage To Stand In Faith While Waiting To Receive Your Miracle. "Finally, my brethren, be strong in the Lord and in the power of His might," (Ephesians 6:10).

Never...Never...NEVER...Doubt The Love Of God For You.

The World's Greatest Miracle Happened 2000 Years Ago. God gave His Son, Jesus, to die on the cross for our sins.

Calvary Was A Miracle.

Calvary Is Your Place Of Qualification.

His mercy and forgiveness is *proof* that He truly cares.

Your Life, Your Health And Your Happiness Matter To Our Lord. "Happy is that people...whose God is the Lord," (Psalm 144:15).

Sickness and evil come from satan. Jesus came to destroy the works of the devil. "The thief cometh not, but for to steal, and to destroy: I am come that they might have life, and that they might have it more abundantly," (John 1:10).

It is not the Will of God that you suffer sickness and die prematurely. Jesus has already defeated early death. "Forasmuch then as the children are partakers of flesh and blood, He also Himself took part of the same; that through death He might destroy him that had the power of death, that is, the devil," (Hebrews 2:14).

God wants you well. The love of Jesus has already paid the price for your healing Miracle. The stripes delivered by the whip of a Roman made Jesus barely recognizable.

Celebrate His Healing Presence Now. "Who His own self bare our sins in His own body on the tree, that we, being dead to sins, should live in righteousness: by Whose stripes ye were healed," (1 Peter 2:24).

God has so much invested in you. Consider this well-known, ancient truth, "For God so loved the world, that He gave His only begotten Son, that whosoever believeth in Him should not perish, but have everlasting life," (John 3:16). The same God who removes the stain of sin from your heart also removes sickness, disease and poverty from your life. Accepting His love for you makes expecting Miracles so much easier.

Reminders That Unlock Your Faith

▶ Miracles are not for the holy.
▶ Miracles are for the *hungry.*
▶ Miracles only happen for the person who believes. So, Believe.
▶ Doubt never produces what you really want.
▶ *Discard Your Doubts.*
▶ Warfare will always surround the *birth* of a Miracle.
▶ *Stir up* your own faith.
▶ Make the extra effort to believe...*just one more time.*
▶ The Grapes of Blessing are not placed within your mouth, but *within your reach.*
▶ *Never* Quit Reaching.

► *Pursuit* Qualifies You For Receiving.

The fact you are reading these words is proof that you qualify for a Miracle. "The Lord is good unto them that wait for Him and the soul that seeketh Him," (Lamentations 3:25).

Reconstruct A More Accurate Picture Of God. God is not a harsh dictator who wants to smash earthlings at the slightest sign of error. Instead, He is a God of Miracles...Love...Compassion...and Healing. "Yea, I have loved thee with an everlasting love...with lovingkindness have I drawn thee," (Jeremiah 31:3).

Invest The Seed Of Time In The Secret Place. "...in Your presence is fullness of joy," (Psalm 19:11). Faith will rise for Miracles as you enjoy your time with Him.

Stay In His Presence Until You Hear His Voice. Hearing His voice will give you the strength you need to call forth your Miracle, "And when He had spoken unto me, I was strengthened," (Daniel 10:19).

You Must Believe In Your Own Worthiness To Receive A Miracle.

RECOMMENDED INVESTMENTS:
B-65   Born to Taste the Grapes (32 pages/$3)
B-69   Wisdom Keys for a Powerful Prayer Life (32 pages/$3)
B-78   The Mentor's Manna on The Secret Place (32 pages/$3)
B-115 Where Miracles Are Born (32 pages/$5)

≈ 5 ≈

You Must Have Confidence In The Character Of God

God Can Be Trusted.

God *Wants* To Be Trusted. Anger and complaining will not attract God. His only pleasure is to be *trusted.* His only pain is to be *doubted.* Your conversation must reveal your trust.

His *Mind* Is Keener Than Yours.

His *Memory* Is Longer Than Yours.

His *Shoulders* Are Bigger Than Yours.

Remember...*The Dominant Difference In People Is Who They Have Chosen To Trust.*

Right Words Can Motivate And Energize You To Believe God For Your Miracle. "A man hath joy by the answer of his mouth: and a word spoken in due season, how good is it!" (Proverbs 15:23).

Faith-Talk Destroys Doubt. "He that keepeth his mouth keepeth his life," (Proverbs 13:3).

Miracles Are Birthed Through Your Words. "Death and life are in the power of the tongue: and they that love it shall eat the fruit thereof," (Proverbs 18:21).

Faith-Words Are Seeds For Wellness In Every Part Of Your Life. "...the tongue of the wise is health," (Proverbs 12:18).

Visualize God stepping into the arena of your life. He is turning the tide in your favor. "Every valley shall be exalted, and every mountain and hill shall be made low: and the crooked shall be made straight, and the rough places plain: And the glory of the Lord shall be revealed, and all flesh shall see it together: for the mouth of the Lord hath spoken it," (Isaiah 4:4-5).

God Is A Blesser.

You Must Have Confidence In The Character Of God.

≈ 6 ≈

You Must Accept And Complete Any Instruction That Authorizes The Release Of Your Miracle

Every Miracle Involves An Instruction.

Jesus Told The Blind Man To Wash The Clay And Spittle From His Eyes. "I must work the works of Him that sent Me, while it is day: the night cometh, when no man can work. As long as I am in the world, I am the light of the world. When He had thus spoken, He spat on the ground, and made clay of the spittle, and He anointed the eyes of the blind man with the clay, And said unto him, Go, wash in the pool of Siloam, (which is by interpretation, Sent.) He went his way therefore, and washed, and came seeing," (John 9:4-7).

Elisha Gave Naaman An Instruction To Dip Seven Times In The Jordan River. "And Elisha sent a messenger unto him, saying, Go and wash in Jordan seven times, and thy flesh shall come again to thee, and thou shalt be clean...Then went he down, and dipped himself seven times in Jordan, according to the saying of the man of God: and his flesh came again like unto the flesh of a little child, and he was clean," (2 Kings 5:10, 14). Naaman went into the Jordan with leprous skin. Naaman came out of the Jordan with skin like a baby...because he obeyed the instruction of a man of

God.

God Gave Joshua Specific Instructions For Subduing Jericho. God told Joshua to instruct Israel to walk around Jericho once daily for six days. On day seven they were to walk around the city walls seven times. "And the Lord said unto Joshua, See, I have given into thine hand Jericho, and the king thereof, and the mighty men of valour. And ye shall compass the city, all ye men of war, and go round about the city once. Thus shalt thou do six days. And seven priests shall bear before the ark seven trumpets of rams' horns: and the seventh day ye shall compass the city seven times, and the priests shall blow with the trumpets," (Josh. 6:2-4).

Obedience Guarantees Rewards. Joshua had been promised that faithfully following the Divine instruction would cause the fortified walls of Jericho to fall. "And it came to pass on the seventh day, that they rose early about the dawning of the day, and compassed the city after the same manner seven times: only on that day they compassed the city seven times. And it came to pass at the seventh time, when the priests blew with the trumpets, Joshua said unto the people, Shout; for the Lord hath given you the city. So the people shouted when the priests blew with the trumpets: and it came to pass, when the people heard the sound of the trumpet, and the people shouted with a great shout, that the wall fell down flat, so that the people went up into the city, every man straight before him, and they took the city," (Joshua 6:15-16, 20).

► *Instructions Decide Seasons.*
► When You Ask God For A Miracle He Will Always Give You An Instruction.
► Your Obedience Is The Only Proof That You

Believe Him.

An Instruction That Changed My Life

My life was changed in Victoria, Texas when I was 21 years old. Famed Missionary, Charles Greenaway, was the Divine channel. Brother Greenaway, a beloved and respected missionary statesman, was raising support for the Missions Department of the Assemblies of God. He shouted an instruction from the pulpit, *"I dare you to prove God."* He explained that the only place God challenged us to *prove* His existence was in Malachi 3...to throw something up toward Heaven and if more came back to you than you threw up...that was proof of His existence.

I listened to his challenge to make a Faith-Promise...a Seed I would sow during the next 12 months. I was broke. I had been an Evangelist for only one year. My first year of evangelism was a financial catastrophe. One month my income was $35. Another month, it was $90.

I owned a 1953 Chevrolet entering my second year of evangelism, 1967. During the month of June, as I recall, I was invited to attend the South Texas District Council of the Assemblies of God.

Nervously trembling, I responded to the message of Brother Greenaway and stood to my feet wondering how I could secure the extra $100...within 12 months. (These days, this sounds like very little. But, at that time it was a huge step of faith because I had *nothing*.)

Yet, the message Brother Greenaway had shared from Leviticus 19:9-10 was burning in my spirit. I knew I had to obey. As I recall this instance, I can almost hear him today…"In the Old Testament, the rich were instructed to leave the corners of their barley or wheat fields for the poor. God promised to bless them if they would sow back and make their corners big to God and the people who were hurting. Your *field* is your *income*. Your *corners* represent your *outgo* to God. If you will increase the size of your corners, God will increase the size of your field, or your income." He asked the question I have never forgotten.

"How big is your corner?"

The trip back to my home that Thursday morning from Victoria to Lake Charles, Louisiana was a very emotional one.

Where on earth was I going to find $100?

The house I was living in was purchased by my father for the grand price of…$150! He had bought *the entire house* for $150 and moved it onto some land he owned. So, I was living in it. My bedroom suite cost a mere $35.

The following Sunday morning, Merle Daley, an old pianist for the Stamps Quartet, stopped by to visit our church. When he finished playing a piano solo for my father's congregation, he stood and spoke.

"Folks, God has been so good to me! Right now my pockets are full of $100 bills!"

I stared wide-eyed.

Suddenly, he looked at me sitting on the far left side of the building.

Then he said, "In fact, God just spoke to me to give one of these $100 bills to Mike!"

Oh, I knew he knew God!

Monday morning, I deposited his gift of $100 into my checking account and promptly wrote a check to the

South Texas District Council of the Assemblies of God to pay my Faith-Promise.

Tuesday morning, I drove to Beeville, Texas to minister at the First Assembly of God Church where James Brothers was the host pastor.

While driving through Beeville, I saw a trailer with a FOR SALE sign on it for $100. It was precisely the very kind of trailer I had wanted to carry my clothes, books and belongings to the meetings. I was sick inside because I had just paid my Faith-Promise...*and no longer had the $100 to purchase the trailer!* It seemed to me that satan whispered to my heart, "See what you could have had if you had not paid your faith-promise!" I agreed, of course.

That night, I went early to the church and sat at the old upright piano on the platform. While practicing before service, a couple walked in. After a few minutes she walked up behind me at the piano and tapped me on the shoulder.

"My husband and I felt impressed to give this to you," she said.

I turned around and looked at one of the most beautiful sights I have ever seen—her check for $150!

I responded excitedly, "This is God, my sister! I saw a small trailer today while driving through town that I desperately wanted that costs $100. Now I have more than enough to buy it."

The next day, Wednesday, I purchased the trailer and had $50 left over. So, I immediately rushed another Seed of $50 to the South Texas District Council of the Assemblies of God. I had already paid my Faith-Promise, but I felt that *anything that works with God that fast...I was determined to work the living daylights out of!*

Wednesday night came. While I was practicing the piano again, the couple walked in with another beautiful check. "We could not sleep last night. The Holy Spirit spoke to our hearts and said we were supposed to buy the trailer for you also. Here's a check for $100 to pay for the trailer."

My Parade of Miracle-Harvests had just been birthed.

Obeying The Voice of The Holy Spirit had activated a collection of Miracles that would change my life forever.

What has God instructed you to do?

Is there a vow you have not paid? "When thou vowest a vow unto God, defer not to pay it; for He hath no pleasure in fools: pay that which thou hast vowed," (Ecclesiastes 5:4).

You Must Accept And Complete Any Instruction That Authorizes The Release Of Your Miracle.

RECOMMENDED INVESTMENTS:
B-15   Seeds of Wisdom on Miracles (32 pages/$3)
B-20   Seeds of Wisdom on Obedience (32 pages/$3)

7

YOU MUST DEVELOP AN ENVIRONMENT OF EXPECTATION AND OBEDIENCE

Expectation Is Proof Of Your Faith.

Obedience births Hope. *Immediately.* Hope is The Entry into the Faith-World. Nothing happens until you unleash Expectation into your environment.

Were you instructed to speak with someone about their soul? "...for the Lord shall greatly bless thee in the land which the Lord thy God giveth thee for an inheritance to possess it: Only if thou carefully hearken unto the voice of the Lord thy God, to observe to do all these commandments which I command thee this day," (Deuteronomy 15:4-5).

The Holy Spirit Is The Master Communicator. The heart cry of Jesus is that we obey The Holy Spirit. "He that hath an ear, let Him hear what the Spirit saith unto the churches," (Revelation 2:7).

Recognition Of The Voice Of The Holy Spirit Can Unlock Waves Of Favor And Blessing.

My Entry Into Christian Television

One afternoon my telephone rang while I was still living in Houston, Texas. It was a dear friend, Roger McDuff. Roger has been a legend in gospel music for many years.

"Mike, while praying, The Holy Spirit spoke to me to ask you to go with me to California. Paul and Jan Crouch head Channel 40 in Santa Ana, California. Have you heard of them?"

I had not.

"If you can purchase your ticket, I would like to introduce you to them. I believe that there is a connection between you and them."

Within days, Paul Crouch had invited me to be a continuous guest on scores and scores of programs. He and Jan sponsored my telecast on their station for over four years. Many miracles occurred. Thousands of people received our ministry. It was astounding.

Roger heard and obeyed The Voice of The Holy Spirit.

I heard and obeyed The Voice of The Holy Spirit.

Paul and Jan Crouch heard and obeyed The Voice of The Holy Spirit.

My life has been a wave of Miracles since that decisive day.

No Miracle Occurs Without Obedience. "But if thou shalt obey His voice, and do all that I speak; then I will be an enemy unto thine enemies, and an adversary until thine adversaries. For Mine Angel shall go before thee," (Exodus 23:22-23). Take this truth deep into your spirit. If you are obedient, God becomes an enemy to your enemies.

God is the enemy of *sickness*...for the Obedient.

God is the enemy of *poverty*...for the Obedient.

God is the enemy of *depression*...for the Obedient.

The Door Of Blessing Is Hinged Upon Obedience.

Have you failed to pay the Holy Tithe to your local

church? Is it reasonable to expect God to give you a Miracle when you are not blessing His house and sustaining His minister? "Will a man rob God? Yet ye have robbed Me. But ye say, Wherein have we robbed Thee? In tithes and offerings. Ye are cursed with a curse: for ye have robbed Me, even this whole nation. Bring ye all the tithes into the storehouse, that there may be meat in Mine house, and prove Me now herewith, saith the Lord of hosts, if I will not open you the windows of heaven, and pour you out a blessing, that there shall not be room enough to receive it," (Malachi 3:8-10).

Miraculous Prosperity Is Directly Linked To Obedience. "If ye be willing and obedient, you will eat the good of the land," (Isaiah 1:19-20).

The Miraculous Provision Of Others May Be Directly Linked To Your Obedience. "For as by one man's disobedience many were made sinners, so by the obedience of one many be made righteous," (Romans 5:19).

Obedience Will Not Be Forced Upon You. "God resisteth the proud, but giveth grace unto the humble. Humble yourselves in the sight of the Lord, and He shall life you up," (James 4:6, 10).

Submission To The Holy Spirit Always Produces Financial Miracles. "And He sought the Lord in the days of Zechariah, who had understanding of the visions of God: and *as long as he sought the Lord,* God made him to prosper," (2 Chronicles 26:5).

Humble Obedience Always Guarantees Uncommon Provision. "By humility and the fear of the Lord are riches, honour and life," (Proverbs 22:4).

When You Come Into Compliance With The Word

Of God, You Qualify For A Miracle. "And I will rebuke the devourer for your sakes, and he shall not destroy the fruits of your ground; neither shall your vine cast her fruit before the time in the field, saith the Lord of hosts," (Malachi 3:11).

God Wants Us To Obey Him In Order To Produce Seasons Of Blessing And Reward In Our Lives. "If ye be willing and obedient, ye shall eat the good of the land," (Isaiah 1:19).

Obedience Is The Golden Bridge To Your Miracle. All the blessings of God are conditioned with obedience. "...if thou shalt hearken diligently to the voice of the Lord thy God," (Deuteronomy 28:1).

Obedience Is The Only Proof That You Really Trust Him. "God is not a man, that He should lie; neither is He the son of man, that He should repent: hath He said, and shall He not do it? Or hath He spoken and shall He not make it good?" (Numbers 23:19).

God Expects Obedience. "My sheep hear My voice, and I know them, and they follow Me," (John 10:27).

Is there any instruction you have left undone? If so, go back and immediately comply with the command of God.

Your Miracle is always dependent upon your obedience. ALWAYS.

Listen for His voice. Obeying it unleashes the flood gates of Expectation. Expectation is the magnet for every desirable event you want to occur in your life.

You Must Develop An Environment Of Expectation And Obedience.

Millionaire-Talk

DR. MIKE MURDOCK

MY GIFT OF APPRECIATION
GIFT of Appreciation
Wisdom Is The Principal Thing

31 Things You Will Need To Become A Millionaire (CD/MT-20)

Topics Include:

▷ *You Will Need Financial Heroes*
▷ *Your Willingness To Negotiate Everything*
▷ *You Must Have The Ability To Transfer Your Enthusiasm, Your Vision To Others*
▷ *Know Your Competition*
▷ *Be Willing To Train Your Team Personally As To Your Expectations*
▷ *Hire Professionals To Do A Professional's Job*

have asked the Lord for 3,000 special partners who will sow an extra Seed of $58 towards he Ministry Outreaches. Your Seed is so appreciated! Remember to request my Gift CD, *31 Things You Will Need To Become A Millionaire,* when you write this week!

Miracle 7 BOOK PAK!

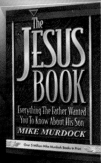

❶ **Dream Seeds**/Book (106pg/B-11/$9)

❷ **Seeds of Wisdom on Favor**/Book (32pg/B-119/$5)

❸ **Seeds of Wisdom on Miracles**/Book (32pg/B-15/$3)

❹ **Seeds of Wisdom on Prayer**/Book (32pg/B-23/$3)

❺ **The Jesus Book**/Book (166pg/B-27/$10)

❻ **The Memory Bible on Miracles**/Book (32pg/B-208/$3)

❼ **The Mentor's Manna on Attitude**/Book (32pg/B-58/$3)

DR. MIKE MURDOCK

The Wisdom Center
Miracle 7 Book Pak!
Only $**30** $36 Value
WBL-24
Wisdom Is The Principal Thing

Add 10% For S/H

Quantity Prices Available Upon Request

**Each Wisdom Book may be purchased separately if so desired.

B **THE WISDOM CENTER** 4051 Denton Highway • Fort Worth, TX 76117
1-817-759-BOOK
1-817-759-0300

─ You Will Love Our Website...! ─
wisdomonline.com

Crisis 7 BOOK PAK!

DR. MIKE MURDOCK

❶ The Survival Bible/<u>Book</u> (248pg/B-29/$10)

❷ Wisdom For Crisis Times/<u>Book</u> (112pg/B-40/$9)

❸ Seeds of Wisdom on Motivating Yourself/<u>Book</u> (32pg/B-171/$5)

❹ Seeds of Wisdom on Overcoming/<u>Book</u> (32pg/B-17/$3)

❺ Seeds of Wisdom on Warfare/<u>Book</u> (32pg/B-19/$3)

❻ Battle Techniques For War-Weary Saints/<u>Book</u> (32pg/B-07/$5)

❼ Seeds of Wisdom on Adversity/<u>Book</u> (32pg/B-21/$3)

The Wisdom Center
Crisis 7 Book Pak!
Only $**30** $38 Value
WBL-25
Wisdom Is The Principal Thing

Add 10% For S/H

DISCOVER   MasterCard   VISA

Quantity Prices Available Upon Request

**Each Wisdom Book may be purchased separately if so desired.

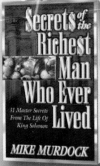

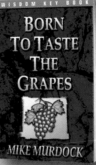

Money 7 BOOK PAK!

1 Secrets of the Richest Man Who Ever Lived/<u>Book</u> (179pg/B-99/$10)

2 The Blessing Bible/<u>Book</u> (252pg/B-28/$10)

3 Born To Taste The Grapes/<u>Book</u> (32pg/B-65/$3)

4 Creating Tomorrow Through Seed-Faith/<u>Book</u> (32pg/B-06/$5)

5 Seeds of Wisdom on Prosperity/<u>Book</u> (32pg/B-22/$3)

6 Seven Obstacles To Abundant Success/<u>Book</u> (32pg/B-64/$3)

7 Ten Lies Many People Believe About Money/<u>Book</u> (32pg/B-04/$5)

DR. MIKE MURDOCK

The Wisdom Center
Money 7 Book Pak!
Only $**30** $39 Value
WBL-30
Wisdom Is The Principal Thing

**Each Wisdom Book may be purchased separately if so desired.

Add 10% For S/H

Career 7

Book Pak For Business People!

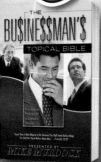

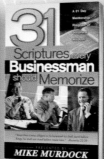
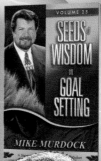

DR. MIKE MURDOCK

❶ **The Businessman's Topical Bible**/<u>Book</u> (384pg/B-33/$10)

❷ **31 Secrets for Career Success**/<u>Book</u> (114pg/B-44/$10)

❸ **31 Scriptures Every Businessman Should Memorize**/<u>Book</u> (32pg/B-141/$3)

❹ **Seeds of Wisdom on Goal-Setting**/<u>Book</u> (32pg/B-127/$5)

❺ **Seeds of Wisdom on Problem-Solving**/<u>Book</u> (32pg/B-118/$5)

❻ **Seeds of Wisdom on Productivity**/<u>Book</u> (32pg/B-137/$5)

❼ **The Mentor's Manna on Achievement**/<u>Book</u> (32pg/B-79/$3)

Each Wisdom Book may be purchased separately if so desired.

The Wisdom Center
Career 7 Book Pak!
Only **$30** $41 Value
WBL-27
Wisdom Is The Principal Thing

Add 10% For S/H

THE WISDOM CENTER 1-817-759-BOOK
4051 Denton Highway • Fort Worth, TX 76117 — 1-817-759-0300

You Will Love Our Website...!
wisdomonline.com

E

101 Wisdom Keys That Have Most Changed My Life.

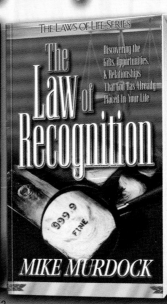

THE LAWS OF LIFE SERIES

The **Law** of **Recognition**

Discovering the Gifts, Opportunities, & Relationships That God Has Already Placed In Your Life

MIKE MURDOCK

TS-42

School of Wisdom #2 Pak!

- ▶ What Attracts Others Toward You
- ▶ The Secret Of Multiplying Your Financial Blessings
- ▶ What Stops The Flow Of Your Faith
- ▶ Why Some Fail And Others Succeed
- ▶ How To Discern Your Life Assignment
- ▶ How To Create Currents Of Favor With Others
- ▶ How To Defeat Loneliness
- ▶ 47 Keys In Recognizing The Mate God Has Approved For You
- ▶ 14 Facts You Should Know About Your Gifts And Talents
- ▶ 17 Important Facts You Should Remember About Your Weakness
- ▶ And Much, Much More...

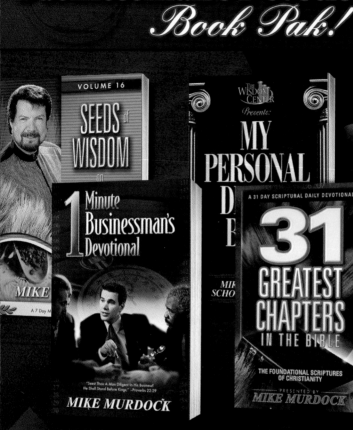

The CRISIS COLLECTION

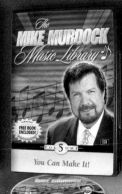

You Get All 6 For One Great Price!

❶ 7 Keys For Surviving A Crisis/<u>DVD</u> (MMPL-04D/$10)

❷ You Can Make It!/<u>Music CD</u> (MMML-05/$10)

❸ Wisdom For Crisis Times/<u>6 Cassettes</u> (TS-40/$30)

❹ Seeds of Wisdom on Overcoming/<u>Book</u> (32pg/B-17/$3)

❺ Seeds of Wisdom on Motivating Yourself/<u>Book</u> (32pg/B-171/$5)

❻ Wisdom For Crisis Times/<u>Book</u> (112pg/B-40/$9)

Also Included... Two Free Bonus Books!

Each Wisdom Product may be purchased separately if so desired.

The Wisdom Center

The Crisis Collection

Only $**40** $67 Value

PAK-16

Wisdom Is The Principal Thing

Add 10% For S/H

THE TURNAROUND Collection

- **BATTLE TECHNIQUES FOR WAR WEARY SAINTS** — WISDOM KEY BOOK — MIKE MURDOCK
- THE *Wisdom* COLLECTOR'S EDITION — THE WISDOM COMMENTARY 1
- **SEEDS of WISDOM** ON OVERCOMING — Mike Murdock
- Volume 2 — The Memory Bible on Healing — 31 Scriptures Every Believer Should Memorize About Healing — PRESENTED BY MIKE MURDOCK
- **HOW TO TURN YOUR MISTAKES INTO MIRACLES** — WISDOM KEY BOOK — MIKE MURDOCK
- The MIKE MURDOCK *Partnership Library* — 7 Keys To Turning Your Life Around — FREE BOOK ENCLOSED! — DVD — VOLUME 3
- The MIKE MURDOCK *Music Library* — FREE BOOK ENCLOSED! — VOLUME 1 — CD — The Sun Will Shine Again

❶ **The Wisdom Commentary Vol. 1**/<u>Book</u> (256pg/52 Topics/B-136/$20)

❷ **Battle Techniques For War-Weary Saints**/<u>Book</u> (32pg/B-07/$5)

❸ **Seeds of Wisdom on Overcoming**/<u>Book</u> (32pg/B-17/$3)

❹ **The Memory Bible on Healing**/<u>Book</u> (32pg/B-196/$3)

❺ **How To Turn Your Mistakes Into Miracles**/<u>Book</u> (32pg/B-56/$5)

❻ **7 Keys To Turning Your Life Around**/<u>DVD</u> (MMPL-03D/$10)

❼ **The Sun Will Shine Again**/<u>Music CD</u> (MMML-01/$10)

**Each Wisdom Product may be purchased separately if so desired.

The Wisdom Center
The Turnaround Collection
Only $**40** $56 Value
PAK-15
Wisdom Is The Principal Thing

Add 10% For S/H

 THE WISDOM CENTER 4051 Denton Highway • Fort Worth, TX 76117 — **1-817-759-BOOK** — **1-817-759-0300**

You Will Love Our Website...! — wisdomonline.com

I

Favor 4!

This Collection Of Wisdom Will Change The Seasons Of Your Life Forever!

1 The School of Wisdom #4 / 31 Keys To Unleashing Uncommon Favor...Tape Series/<u>6 Cassettes</u> (TS-44/$30)

2 The Hidden Power Of Right Words... *The Wisdom Center Pastoral Library*/<u>CD</u> (WCPL-27/$10)

3 Seeds of Wisdom on Favor/<u>Book</u> (32pg/B-119/$5)

4 Seeds of Wisdom on Obedience/<u>Book</u> (32pg/B-20/$3)

**Each Wisdom Product may be purchased separately if so desired.

J THE WISDOM CENTER
4051 Denton Highway • Fort Worth, TX 76117
1-817-759-BOOK
1-817-759-0300
You Will Love Our Website...!
wisdomonline.com

Financial $ecrets.

The Wisdom Center
Buy One... Receive The Second One FREE!
Wisdom Is The Principal Thing

31 REASON$** PEOPLE DO NOT RECEIVE THEIR **FINANCIAL HARVE$T — THE 31 DAY MENTORSHIP PROGRAM — MIKE MURDOCK

VIDEO — **7 KEYS to 1000 TIMES MORE** — *The Lord God Of Your Fathers Make You A Thousand Times So Many More As You Are, And Bless You, As He Hath Promised You! Deuteronomy 1:11* — MIKE MURDOCK

Your Financial World Will Change Forever.

Video 2-Pak!

8 Scriptural Reasons You Should Pursue Financial Prosperity

The Secret Prayer Key You Need When Making A Financial Request To God

The Weapon Of Expectation And The 5 Miracles It Unlocks

How To Discern Those Who Qualify To Receive Your Financial Assistance

How To Predict The Miracle Moment God Will Schedule Your Financial Breakthrough

Habits Of Uncommon Achievers

The Greatest Success Law I Ever Discovered

How To Discern Your Place Of Assignment, The Only Place Financial Provision Is Guaranteed

3 Secret Keys In Solving Problems For Others

The Wisdom Center
Video 2-Pak!
Only $30 $60 Value
VIPAK-01
Wisdom Is The Principal Thing

Add 10% For S/H

*Each Wisdom Product may be purchased separately if so desired.

THE WISDOM CENTER
4051 Denton Highway • Fort Worth, TX 76117

1-817-759-BOOK
1-817-759-0300

You Will Love Our Website...!
wisdomonline.com

K

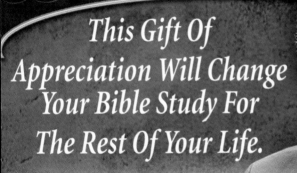

This Gift Of Appreciation Will Change Your Bible Study For The Rest Of Your Life.

MY GIFT OF APPRECIATION
Celebrating Your Sponsorship Seed of $1,000 For The Prayer Center & TV Studio Complex
Wisdom Is The Principal Thing
B-235

Spirit Music.

The Mike Murdock Music Library

LOVE SONGS TO THE HOLY SPIRIT

Written In The Secret Place

TS-59

THE HOLY SPIRIT HANDBOOK
What You Need To Know About Your Daily Companion, The Holy Spirit

MURDOCK

The Wisdom Center
Free Book ENCLOSED!
B-100 ($10 Value)
Wisdom Is The Principal Thing

Songs...

1. A Holy Place
2. Anything You Want
3. Everything Comes From You
4. Fill This Place With Your Presence
5. First Thing Every Morning
6. Holy Spirit, I Want To Hear You
7. Holy Spirit, Move Again
8. Holy Spirit, You Are Enough
9. I Don't Know What I Would Do Without You
10. I Let Go (Of Anything That Stops Me)
11. I'll Just Fall On You
12. I Love You, Holy Spirit
13. I'm Building My Life Around You
14. I'm Giving Myself To You
15. I'm In Love! I'm In Love!
16. I Need Water (Holy Spirit, You're My Well)
17. In The Secret Place

18. In Your Presence, I'm Always Changed
19. In Your Presence (Miracles Are Born)
20. I've Got To Live In Your Presence
21. I Want To Hear Your Voice
22. I Will Do Things Your Way
23. Just One Day At A Time
24. Meet Me In The Secret Place
25. More Than Ever Before
26. Nobody Else Does What You Do
27. No No Walls!
28. Nothing Else Matters Anymore (Since I've Been In The Presence Of You Lord)
29. Nowhere Else
30. Once Again You've Answered
31. Only A Fool Would Try (To Live Without You)
32. Take Me Now
33. Teach Me How To Please You

34. There's No Place I'd Rather
35. Thy Word Is All That Matters
36. When I Get In Your Presence
37. You're The Best Thing (That' Ever Happened To Me)
38. You Are Wonderful
39. You've Done It Once
40. You Keep Changing Me
41. You Satisfy

The Wisdom Center
6 Tapes / Only $30*
PAK007
Wisdom Is The Principal Thing

Add 10% For S/H

**Each Wisdom Product may be purchased separately if so desired.

 THE WISDOM CENTER 4051 Denton Highway • Fort Worth, TX 76117

1-817-759-BOOK
1-817-759-0300

You Will Love Our Website...!
wisdomonline.com

N

YOUR ASSIGNMENT IS YOUR DISTINCTION FROM OTHERS.

Assignment 4 Book Pak!

Uncommon Wisdom For Discovering Your Life Assignment.

Buy 3 Books & Get The 4th Book Free!

❶ The Dream & The Destiny
Vol 1/<u>Book</u> (164 pg/B-74/$10)

❷ The Anointing & The Adversity
Vol 2/<u>Book</u> (192 pg/B-75/$10)

❸ The Trials & The Triumphs
Vol 3/<u>Book</u> (160 pg/B-97/$10)

❹ The Pain & The Passion
Vol 4/<u>Book</u> (144 pg/B-98/$10)

**Each Wisdom Book may be purchased separately if so desired.

The Wisdom Center
Assignment 4 Book Pak!
Only $**30** $40 Value
WBL-14
Wisdom Is The Principal Thing

Add 10% For S/H

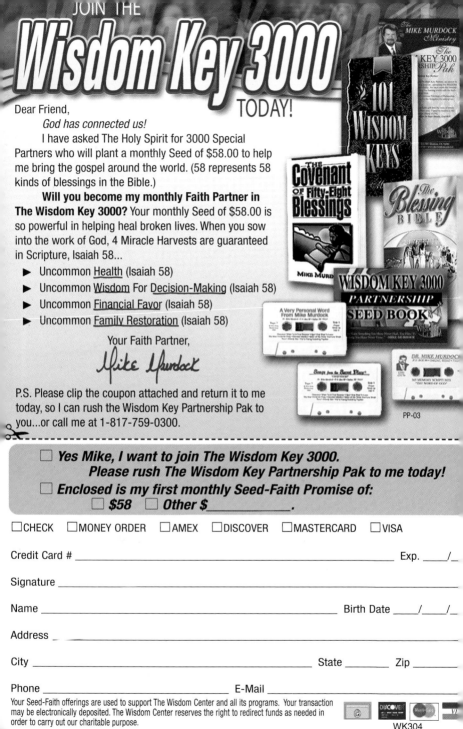

JOIN THE

Wisdom Key 3000 TODAY!

The MIKE MURDOCK Ministry

The KEY 3000 SHIP Pak

Dear Friend,

God has connected us!

I have asked The Holy Spirit for 3000 Special Partners who will plant a monthly Seed of $58.00 to help me bring the gospel around the world. (58 represents 58 kinds of blessings in the Bible.)

Will you become my monthly Faith Partner in The Wisdom Key 3000? Your monthly Seed of $58.00 is so powerful in helping heal broken lives. When you sow into the work of God, 4 Miracle Harvests are guaranteed in Scripture, Isaiah 58...

► Uncommon <u>Health</u> (Isaiah 58)
► Uncommon <u>Wisdom</u> For <u>Decision-Making</u> (Isaiah 58)
► Uncommon <u>Financial Favor</u> (Isaiah 58)
► Uncommon <u>Family Restoration</u> (Isaiah 58)

Your Faith Partner,

Mike Murdock

P.S. Please clip the coupon attached and return it to me today, so I can rush the Wisdom Key Partnership Pak to you...or call me at 1-817-759-0300.

PP-03

☐ *Yes Mike, I want to join The Wisdom Key 3000.*
  Please rush The Wisdom Key Partnership Pak to me today!
☐ *Enclosed is my first monthly Seed-Faith Promise of:*
    ☐ *$58* ☐ *Other $_____.*

☐ CHECK   ☐ MONEY ORDER   ☐ AMEX   ☐ DISCOVER   ☐ MASTERCARD   ☐ VISA

Credit Card # _____ Exp. ____/_

Signature _____

Name _____ Birth Date ____/____/_

Address _ _____

City _____ State _____ Zip _____

Phone _____ E-Mail _____

Your Seed-Faith offerings are used to support The Wisdom Center and all its programs. Your transaction may be electronically deposited. The Wisdom Center reserves the right to redirect funds as needed in order to carry out our charitable purpose.

WK304

THE WISDOM CENTER 4051 Denton Highway Fort Worth TX, 76117

1-817-759-BOOK
1-817-759-0300

You Will Love Our Website...!
wisdomonline.com